Amalfi Coast

in Your Pocket!

*Your Essential Portable Travel Guide
to the Amalfi Coast and Beyond...*

From Food to Art and the Most Scenic,
Secret Landscapes

Michael J. Nicholson

TABLE OF CONTENTS

MAP OF THE
AMALFI COAST

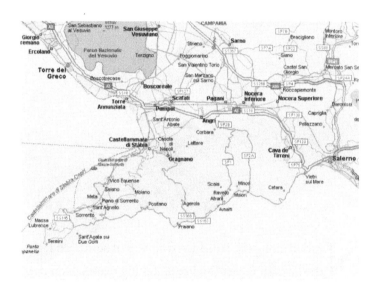

INTRODUCTION

Nestled along the sun-kissed shores of southern Italy, the Amalfi Coast is a breathtaking destination that promises to take your breath away. With its picturesque cliffside towns, sparkling turquoise waters, and mouthwatering cuisine, it's no wonder that travelers from around the world flock to this stunning region year-round. Whether you're seeking a romantic getaway, an adventure-filled trip, or simply a chance to soak up some Mediterranean sun, the Amalfi Coast offers something for everyone. From the winding streets of Positano to the historic charm of Amalfi town, prepare to be swept away by the beauty, culture, and enchantment of this Italian gem. So pack your bags, grab your essentials, and get ready to set on a journey you'll never forget - Welcome to the Amalfi Coast!

CHAPTER 1

BEFORE YOU GO!

You must be super excited to finally be able to visit your dream destination or to cross the Amalfi Coast off your bucket list, but amid all this excitement, don't forget to prepare yourself for what comes next. If this is your first ever visit to this gorgeous coastline, then there are a few pointers that you need to consider first before you go ahead and buy your tickets or apply for your visa.

Decide On The Best Time To Visit:

The Amalfi Coast is a truly magical destination that's worth visiting at any time of year, but choosing the best time to go can make all the difference in your experience. If you're a sun-seeker and love the energy of a bustling crowd, then the high season (June to September) will definitely be your cup of tea. Imagine soaking up the Mediterranean sun, sipping cocktails on the beach, and dancing the night away in one of the Coast's famous nightclubs. If you like a more laid-back vibe, the season April to May or October to November is perfect for you. You'll still enjoy mild temperatures, but with fewer tourists, you'll be able to truly take in the breathtaking views without feeling overwhelmed. Hiking enthusiasts will love the cooler weather and blooming nature during the spring and fall seasons. Whichever season you choose, you're sure to be charmed by the vibrant colors of the towns, the delicious cuisine, and the warm hospitality of the locals.

Choose Your Base-The Place To Stay:

With so many picturesque towns and villages to choose from, deciding on a base can be a tough decision. But fear not, as I'm here to guide you through this exciting process! Whether you're a fan of bustling towns with plenty of amenities or prefer quieter, more authentic experiences, the Amalfi Coast has something for everyone. Picture yourself sipping lemonade in Positano's colorful streets or exploring the hidden gems of Furore. Are you a foodie? Sorrento's exquisite cuisine will undoubtedly satisfy your taste buds. Do you want to explore the region beyond the Amalfi Coast? Salerno's accessibility will make your travels much more comfortable. Whatever your preference, rest assured that you'll be captivated by the beauty and history of this enchanting region.

Book Accommodations:

Booking accommodations on the Amalfi Coast before arrival is essential to ensure a stress-free and enjoyable trip. To start, it's important to research the different towns and villages in the region and identify which one best suits your needs and preferences. Once you've made your decision, look for accommodation options in the area that match your budget, such as hotels, beds, breakfasts, or apartments.

When booking your accommodations, pay attention to the amenities offered, such as Wi-Fi, air conditioning, and parking. Check if the property is located near restaurants, shops, and public transportation, as this can greatly enhance your experience. It's also recommended to read reviews from previous guests to gain insight into the quality of the property and the service provided. This can help you avoid any shocking surprises during your stay.

To book your accommodations, you can visit popular travel websites like Booking.com, Expedia, or TripAdvisor or contact the property directly through their website or phone number. Make sure to check the cancellation policy before making a reservation in case your plans change. Booking accommodations in advance will not only save you time and money but also ensure that you have a comfortable and enjoyable stay on the Amalfi Coast. So don't wait till the eleventh hour – start planning and booking your accommodations today!

Plan Your Itinerary:

As there are just so many things to see and do on the Amalfi Coast, it's a good idea to plan your itinerary in advance. Some popular activities include visiting the towns of Positano, Amalfi, and Ravello, hiking the Path of the Gods, taking a boat tour of the Coast, and visiting the ancient city of Pompeii. Planning your itinerary for the Amalfi Coast is essential to make the most out of this trip. With its stunning views and rich cultural heritage, the region offers an abundance of activities and sights that cater to a variety of interests.

Identify your priorities: Whether it's visiting historic landmarks, indulging in delicious cuisine, or enjoying the natural scenery, identifying your priorities will help you narrow down your options.

Research the different towns and villages: The Amalfi Coast boasts several charming towns and villages, each with its own unique character and attractions. Research the different areas and identify which ones align with your interests and priorities. The upcoming chapters of this travel guide will definitely help you decide which towns and special places you would want to add to your itinerary.

Determine the length of your stay: The length of your stay will determine how much you can fit into your itinerary. Keep in mind that the Amalfi Coast is best experienced at a leisurely pace, so it's better to focus on a few key activities rather than trying to cram too much into your schedule.

Create a rough itinerary: Once you've identified your priorities and researched the different areas, create a rough itinerary that outlines the activities and sights you want to visit each day. Be sure to factor in travel time and any necessary reservations, such as for restaurants or tours.

Be flexible: While having a rough itinerary is helpful, it's also important to be flexible and open to unexpected opportunities. Leave room for spontaneity and take advantage of any recommendations from locals or other travelers.

Pack appropriately: The Amalfi Coast has a Mediterranean climate, with hot summers and mild winters. Be sure to pack clothing appropriate for the season, such as lightweight fabrics and sandals for summer, as well as a light jacket or sweater for cooler evenings. Another important consideration is footwear; the region's steep hills and cobblestone streets can be challenging to navigate in high heels or uncomfortable shoes. As such, it's recommended to bring comfortable walking shoes or sneakers for sightseeing and exploring. Given the abundance of stunning beaches and swimming spots, it's also worth packing swimwear and a towel. To protect your skin from the intense Mediterranean sun, bring sunscreen with a high SPF and a hat. Finally, many of the towns and villages on the Amalfi Coast are pedestrian-only, so it's important to pack light and avoid bringing bulky luggage. Consider bringing a backpack or small suitcase that is easy to carry around. Other essentials to pack include a camera, adapter plugs for electronics, a reusable water bottle, and any necessary medications.

Learn Some Italian:

While it's not necessary to learn Italian before visiting the Amalfi Coast, it can certainly enhance your experience and make your trip more enjoyable. Many locals in the area speak some English, especially those working in the tourism industry, but knowing some basic Italian can help you communicate more effectively and connect with the local culture. Learning a few key phrases like "ciao" (hello), "Grazie" (thank you), and "scusi" (excuse me) can go a long way in making a good impression and showing respect to the locals. It can also be helpful to learn some food-related terms if you're interested in trying the local cuisine, such as "pasta" (pasta), "pizza" (pizza), and "gelato" (ice cream).

Additionally, learning about the history and culture of the region can deepen your appreciation of the sights and attractions. You can consider taking an Italian language course before your trip or downloading a language learning app to practice while on the go.

CHAPTER 2

GETTING AROUND ON AMALFI COAST

After landing in Italy and leaving the airport, you are going to require some form of transport to take you to the hotel and to move around from place to place. Since Amalfi Coast is a popular tourist destination, it offers all sorts of transport services for people to roam around easily. From car rentals to public buses, ferries, taxis, and private transport services, you can avail any facility to move around. Here are some of the most common transportation options available in the region:

Rental Cars

Car rental is a popular option for visitors to the Amalfi Coast who want the flexibility to explore the region at their own pace. Here are some car rental options on the Amalfi Coast:

Local Car Rental Companies

There are many local car rental companies that operate in the Amalfi Coast region. These companies offer a range of vehicle types, from compact cars to larger vehicles that can accommodate families or groups. Some popular local rental companies include:

- Europcar
- Hertz
- Avis
- Sixt
- Budget
- Auto Europe
- Maggiore
- Locauto

These companies offer a range of vehicle types, from economy cars to luxury vehicles, as well as additional services such as GPS navigation, child seats, and insurance coverage. Visitors can book a rental car online in advance or visit a rental car office in person to arrange a rental. It is important to note that the coastal roads on the Amalfi Coast can be narrow and winding, and parking can be difficult and expensive in some towns. Visitors should also be aware of the limited parking options and potential traffic congestion during peak season. It is recommended to book a car with a GPS navigation system to help navigate the roads.

Online Car Rental Booking Websites

Many online car rental booking websites offer rental cars on the Amalfi Coast. These websites allow you to compare prices and vehicle types across multiple rental companies. Some popular online booking websites include

- Expedia
- Kayak
- Rentalcars.com.

Rental Cars From Naples Or Salerno

Visitors to the Amalfi Coast can also rent a car from Naples or Salerno, which are both major transportation hubs. This is a good option for visitors who are arriving by plane or train. There are various rental car companies located at the Naples and Salerno airports, as well as in the city centers. It is important to note that the coastal roads on the Amalfi Coast can be narrow and winding, and parking can be difficult and expensive in some towns. Visitors should also be aware of the limited parking options and potential traffic congestion during peak season. It is recommended to book a car with a GPS navigation system to help navigate the roads.

Public Buses

Public buses are a popular and affordable option for getting around the Amalfi Coast. The main bus company in the area is SITA, which operates a network of bus routes that connect the coastal towns and villages of the Amalfi Coast. Additionally, the buses come equipped with storage space below to accommodate your luggage. The frequency of bus service is typically every 15-30 minutes.

Routes: SITA operates several bus routes that run between the main towns of the Amalfi Coast, including Amalfi, Positano, Ravello, Sorrento, and Salerno. There are also buses that connect the smaller villages in the area.

Frequency: The frequency of buses can vary depending on the time of year and the route. During the peak tourist season, buses can be very crowded and may run less frequently due to traffic congestion.

Tickets: Bus tickets can be purchased at ticket booths, bars, and newsstands and must be validated on the bus. It is important to keep the ticket with you for the duration of the journey, as bus inspectors may check tickets at any time.

Schedules: Bus schedules can be found at bus stops, tourist information centers, and on the SITA website. It is recommended to check the schedule in advance, as buses may run less frequently or have different schedules on weekends and holidays.

Fares: Bus fares vary depending on the distance traveled and the route. The cost of a one-way ticket between two towns on the Amalfi Coast ranges from around €1.50 to €5.50. Visitors can also purchase multi-day tickets or passes that offer discounts on bus travel.

Ferry

Ferries operate between many of the towns along the Amalfi Coast, providing scenic views of the coastline from the water. This is a great way to avoid the narrow and winding roads and also to reach some of the smaller coastal towns. Ferries are a convenient and scenic way to travel between the towns and villages of the Amalfi Coast. The ferry service on the Amalfi Coast is operated by several companies, including:

Travelmar: Operates ferry services between Amalfi, Positano, Salerno, and Capri, as well as other destinations in the region.

Alilauro: Offers ferry services between Sorrento, Positano, Amalfi, and Salerno.

NLG: Provides ferry services between Salerno, Amalfi, and Positano.

Visitors can bring luggage on the ferry but should be aware that space may be limited. Some ferry companies charge an additional fee for luggage.

Train

To reach Sorrento, you need to take a train to Naples Central Station, followed by a smaller, local train. If Sorrento is your final destination, then your journey ends here. However, if you need to travel to towns further along the Coast, then a taxi would be your best option. To get from Sorrento to Positano, a taxi ride would cost approximately €40. For each subsequent city along the Coast, you should budget an additional €10 to €15. The entire train journey to Sorrento should take approximately 2.5 hours.

Taxis

Uber services are not available on Amalfi Coast. Taxis are available, but they can be expensive. From Sorrento to

Ravello, taxis are readily available all along the Coast. Pricing for taxi rides varies greatly depending on your destination, but anticipate a minimum fare of €40 to travel from Sorrento to Positano. If you have excess luggage or more than two people in the taxi, the cost may increase.

While the advantages of taking a taxi are clear - you have the freedom to travel without waiting for others and can reach your destination quickly - keep in mind that traffic can be extremely heavy, particularly during the summer and on weekends. As a result, your journey may take nearly as long as if you were traveling by bus. Under no circumstances should you attempt to negotiate a fare with the taxi driver. Always insist on using the meter since bargaining over price will nearly always result in a loss for you.

Private Transfers

Private transfers can be arranged in advance and are a convenient option for visitors who prefer not to drive or navigate public transportation. Private transfers can be arranged from airports, train stations, and hotels.

It is important to note that the Amalfi Coast is a popular tourist destination, so transportation options can be crowded during peak seasons. It is recommended to plan ahead and book transportation in advance when possible.

CHAPTER 3

WHERE TO STAY?

Your next big step in this plan is to book a place to stay. Since you will be moving around from town to town on Amalfi Coast, you need a detailed guide of all the different types of accommodation options you can avail throughout the Coast. As I said before, it is a major tourist attraction, so this part of Italy is flooded with lots of hotels, hostels, and apartments. You can pick and book a room in any of them depending on your budget and the availability of the rooms. It is advised to make reservations before reaching Italy, especially if you are planning to visit during the peak season; otherwise, you will end up running from hotel to hotel in search of a decent room to stay.

LUXURY HOTELS

The Amalfi Coast is known for its luxury hotels, which offer top-notch amenities, stunning views, and impeccable service. Many of these hotels are housed in historic villas and feature elegant decor and top-of-the-line facilities. The Amalfi Coast in Italy is known for its luxurious accommodations, with many high-end hotels offering stunning views, elegant decor, and top-notch amenities. Here are some of the best luxury hotels in the area:

Belmond Hotel Caruso, Ravello

Address: Piazza S. Giovanni del Toro, 2, 84010 Ravello SA, Italy

Opening hours & days: 24 hrs. (Monday to Sunday)

Map Coordinates: 40°39′05″N 14°36′47″E

This iconic hotel is housed in a restored 11th-century palace and offers panoramic views of the coastline. The hotel has elegant rooms and suites, a spa, an outdoor pool, and gardens.

Monastero Santa Rosa, Conca Dei Marini

Address: Via Roma, 2, 84010 Conca dei Marini SA, Italy

Opening hours & days: 24 hrs. (Monday to Sunday)

Map Coordinates: 40° 37′ 14.61″ N 14° 34′ 38.65″ E

This former monastery has been transformed into a luxury hotel featuring 20 rooms and suites with sea views, a Michelin-starred restaurant, an infinity pool, and a spa.

Hotel Santa Caterina, Amalfi

Address: Via Mauro Comite, 9, 84011 Amalfi SA, Italy

Opening hours & days: 24 hrs. (Monday to Sunday)

Map Coordinates: 40° 37′ 46.16″ N 14° 35′ 34.09″ E

This family-owned hotel is located on a cliff overlooking the sea and features elegant rooms and suites, a private beach, an outdoor pool, and gardens.

Palazzo Avino, Ravello

Address: Via S. Giovanni del Toro, 28, 84010 Ravello SA, Italy

Opening hours & days: 24 hrs. (Monday to Sunday)

Map Coordinates: 40.067790 °N 15.705760 °E

This historical hotel is housed in a restored 12th-century villa and offers luxurious rooms and suites with sea views, a Michelin-starred restaurant, a spa, and a rooftop terrace.

Hotel Villa Cimbrone, Ravello

Address: Via Santa Chiara, 26, 84010 Ravello SA, Italy

Opening hours & days: 24 hrs. (Monday to Sunday)

Map Coordinates: 40.6441° N, 14.6110° E

This elegant hotel is housed in a historic villa with stunning gardens and features luxurious rooms and suites, a Michelin-starred restaurant, an outdoor pool, and a spa.

Le Sirenuse, Positano

Address: Le Sirenuse. Via Cristoforo Colombo, 30 · 84017 Positano (SA) Italy

Opening hours & days: 24 hrs. (Monday to Sunday)

Map Coordinates: 40.6288° N, 14.4876° E

This iconic hotel is located in the heart of Positano and features elegant rooms and suites with sea views, a Michelin-starred restaurant, an outdoor pool, and a spa.

Grand Hotel Excelsior Vittoria, Sorrento

Address: Piazza Torquato Tasso, 34, 80067 Sorrento NA, Italy

Opening hours & days: 24 hrs. (Monday to Sunday)

Map Coordinates: -38.443360 latitude, 146.386330 longitude

This historic hotel is located in the town of Sorrento and features elegant rooms and suites, a private beach, an outdoor pool, and gardens.

BOUTIQUE HOTELS

These smaller, independent hotels offer a more personalized experience than larger chain hotels. They often have unique decor and architecture and may be located in historic buildings. The Amalfi Coast in Italy is home to several boutique hotels which offer unique and intimate accommodations for visitors.

Villa Piedimonte, Ravello

Address: Via della Repubblica, 1, 84010 Ravello SA, Italy

Opening hours & days: 24 hrs. (Monday to Sunday)

Map Coordinates: 33.902560 latitudes, -117.785470 longitude

This elegant hotel is housed in a restored 19th-century villa and features just ten rooms and suites with sea views. The hotel also offers an outdoor pool, gardens, and a restaurant.

Casa Angelina, Praiano

Address: Via Gennaro Capriglione, 147, 84010 Praiano SA, Italy

Opening hours & days: 24 hrs. (Monday to Sunday)

Map Coordinates: 40.6145185, 14.5217157

This minimalist hotel is located on a cliff overlooking the sea and features 39 rooms and suites with contemporary decor. The hotel also offers an outdoor pool, spa, and restaurant.

Villa Treville, Positano

Address: Via Arienzo, 30, 84017 Positano SA, Italy

Opening hours & days: 24 hrs. (Monday to Sunday)

Map Coordinates: Latitude: 45.0978, Longitude: 8.36062

This luxurious hotel is located on a private estate and features just 15 rooms and suites with sea views. The hotel also offers an outdoor pool, private beach, and restaurant.

II San Pietro Di Positano, Positano

Address: Il San Pietro di Positano Via Laurito, 2 – 84017 Positano (SA), Italy

Opening hours & days: 24 hrs. (Monday to Sunday)

Map Coordinates: 40.6232° N, 14.5038° E

This iconic hotel is located on a cliff overlooking the sea and features just 57 rooms and suites with sea views. The hotel also offers a private beach, outdoor pool, spa, and restaurant.

Hotel Villa Franca, Positano

Address: Viale Pasitea, 318, 84017 Positano SA, Italy

Opening hours & days: 24 hrs. (Monday to Sunday)

Map Coordinates: 40°37'44"N 14°28'58"E

This elegant hotel is located in the heart of Positano and features 38 rooms and suites with sea views. The hotel also offers an outdoor pool, rooftop terrace, and restaurant.

Casa Privata, Praiano

Address: Via Rezzola, 41, 84010 Praiano SA, Italy

Opening hours & days: 24 hrs. (Monday to Sunday)

Map Coordinates: Lat. 45°,58',17", N – Long. 9°,15', 17", E

This intimate hotel is located in a 17th-century villa and features just four rooms with sea views. The hotel also offers a private beach, outdoor pool, and restaurant.

Palazzo Marzoli Resort, Minoris

Address: Via G. Marconi, 334, 84017 Positano SA, Italy

Opening hours & days: 24 hrs. (Monday to Sunday)

Map Coordinates: 40.6297° N, 14.4816° E

This historic hotel is located in the town of Minori and features 13 rooms and suites with sea views. The hotel also offers an outdoor pool, gardens, and a restaurant.

BED AND BREAKFASTS

If you're looking for a more intimate, homey experience, a bed, and breakfast may be a good option. These small lodgings often offer home-cooked breakfasts and personalized service. The Amalfi Coast in Italy is home to many charming bed and breakfasts that offer cozy and comfortable accommodations for visitors.

Villa Maria Antonietta, Sorrento

Address: Via Cristoforo Colombo, 41, 84017 Positano SA, Italy

Opening hours & days: Check-in. 2:00 PM 7:30 PM · Check-out. 8:00 AM 10:30 AM

Map Coordinates: 45°3'32.4"N 7°42'23.0"E

This charming bed and breakfast is located in the town of Sorrento and features just six rooms with sea views. The hotel also offers a terrace, gardens, and a restaurant.

Casa Mazzola, Sant'Agata Sui Due Golfi

Address: Via Nastro D'Argento, 35, 80065 Sant'Agnello NA, Italy

Opening hours & days: 8 am–11 pm (Monday to Sunday)

Map Coordinates: 42.298° N, 9.311° E

This cozy bed and breakfast is located in the village of Sant'Agata sui Due Golfi and features just four rooms with sea views. The hotel also offers a terrace and gardens.

La Moresca, Praiano

Address: P.zza Moressa, 1, 84010 Praiano SA, Ital

Opening hours & days: 1 pm–10 pm (Monday to Sunday)

Map Coordinates: 43.8931° N, 10.7897° E

This intimate bed and breakfast is located in the village of Praiano and features just seven rooms with sea views. The hotel also offers a terrace, gardens, and a restaurant.

II Ducato Di Ravello, Ravello

Address: Piazza Duomo, 84010 Ravello SA, Italy

Opening hours & days: 24 hrs. (Monday to Sunday)

Map Coordinates: 40.6496° N, 14.6104° E

This charming bed and breakfast is located in the town of Ravello and features just four rooms with sea views. The hotel also offers a terrace, gardens, and a restaurant.

Casa Pendola, Positano

Address: Via Pendola, 19, 80051 Agerola NA, Italy

Opening hours & days: 24 hrs. (Monday to Sunday)

Map Coordinates: 40.6274° N, 14.5353° E

This cozy bed and breakfast is located in the heart of Positano and features just three rooms with sea views. The hotel also offers a terrace and gardens.

Villa La Tartana, Amalfi

Address: Vicolo Vito Savino, 4/6/8, 84017 Positano SA, Italy

Opening hours & days: 24 hrs. (Monday to Sunday)

Map Coordinates: 40.6285° N, 14.4871° E

This charming bed and breakfast is located in the town of Amalfi and features just seven rooms with sea views. The hotel also offers a terrace, gardens, and a restaurant.

AGRITURISMI

These farm-stay accommodations offer a unique way to experience the Amalfi Coast. They often feature rustic decor and home-cooked meals made with fresh, local ingredients. Agriturismi, or farm stays, offer visitors the opportunity to experience the region's rural charm and agricultural heritage. Here are some Agriturismis in the Amalfi Coast region:

Agriturismo Ii Campanile, Tramonti

Address: Via Pioppi, 84010 Loc. Annunziata SA, Italy

Opening hours & days: 8 am–10:30 pm (Monday to Sunday)

Map Coordinates: 42°53'12.6"N 11°56'33.9"E

This farm stay is located in the town of Tramonti and offers rooms and apartments with views of the surrounding vineyards and mountains. The farm produces its own wine and olive oil, and guests can enjoy tastings and tours.

Agriturismo Mare E Monti, Tramonti

Address: Via Trugnano, 3, 84010 Tramonti SA, Italy

Opening hours & days: 24 hrs. (Monday to Sunday)

Map Coordinates: 40.6277° N, 14.5742° E

This farm stay is also located in Tramonti and offers rooms and apartments with views of the surrounding mountains and sea. The farm produces its own wine, olive oil, and vegetables, and guests can enjoy meals made with fresh ingredients.

Agriturismo Sant'alfonso, Maiori

Address: Via S. Alfonso, 6, 84010 Furore SA, Italy

Opening hours & days: 24 hrs. (Monday to Sunday)

Map Coordinates: 40.6202° N, 14.5411° E

This farm stay is located in the town of Maiori and offers rooms and apartments with views of the surrounding lemon groves and sea. The farm produces its own Limoncello, and guests can enjoy tastings and tours.

Agriturismo Villa Maria, Ravello

Address: Via Pioppi, 84010 Minori SA, Italy

Opening hours & days: 24 hrs. (Monday to Sunday)

Map Coordinates: 40.6544° N, 14.6290° E

This farm stay is located in the town of Ravello and offers rooms and apartments with views of the surrounding mountains and sea. The farm produces its own wine and olive oil, and guests can enjoy tastings and tours.

Agriturismo La Selva, Cetara

Address: Località Petrellosa, 80, 84013 Cava de' Tirreni SA, Italy

Opening hours & days: 7:30 am–11:45 pm (Monday to Sunday)

Map Coordinates: 43.3411° N, 11.2673° E

This farm stay is located in the town of Cetara and offers rooms and apartments with views of the surrounding mountains and sea. The farm produces its own olive oil, and guests can enjoy tastings and tours.

Agriturismo La Palombara, Positano

Address: Via Scraio, 23, 80069 Vico Equense NA, Italy

Opening hours & days: 10 am–7 pm (Monday to Sunday)

Map Coordinates: 42° 4' 0" N, 12° 46' 0" E

This farm stay is located in the town of Positano and offers rooms and apartments with views of the surrounding mountains and sea. The farm produces its own olive oil, and guests can enjoy tastings and tours.

GLAMPING

For a more adventurous stay, glamping (or glamorous camping) is an option on the Amalfi Coast. Tents or cabins with comfortable beds and other amenities are set up in scenic locations, allowing guests to get closer to nature while still enjoying the comforts of a hotel. While glamping options are relatively limited on the Amalfi Coast, there are a few locations that offer a unique way to experience the area's stunning natural beauty. Here are some of the glamping options on the Amalfi Coast:

Eco Glamping Sant'alfonso

Address: Via S. Alfonso, 6, 84010 Furore SA, Italy

Opening hours & days: 24 hrs. (Monday to Sunday)

Map Coordinates: 40.0737° N, 15.9216° E

This glamping site is located in the town of Scala, near the historic town of Ravello. The site features eco-friendly tents with comfortable beds and solar-powered lighting, as well as shared bathroom facilities. Guests can enjoy stunning views of the coastline from the site's terrace and can participate in activities such as yoga, hiking, and cooking classes.

Amalfi Coast Glamping

Address: Amalfi Coast Glamour Camping Via Diego Taiani 26 - 84010 Maiori (SA)

Opening hours & days: 24 hrs. (Monday to Sunday)

Map Coordinates: Latitude 40.7041 - Longitude 14.6442

This glamping site is located in the town of Tramonti, in the hills above the Amalfi Coast. The site features stylish tents with private bathrooms and outdoor showers, as well as a swimming pool, hot tub, and restaurant.

CHAPTER 4

PLACES FOR SIGHTSEEING

Whether you are a history buff, a beach bum, a foodie, or a nature lover, there is something for everyone in this stunning region. Start by visiting Positano, the most famous and picturesque village on the Amalfi Coast, known for its colorful houses and beautiful views. You can also explore Amalfi, the largest town in the region, famous for its lemon groves, limoncello production, and notable landmarks, such as the Duomo di Sant'Andrea. Another way to appreciate the beauty of the Amalfi Coast is by taking a boat tour and sailing along the Coast, stopping at secluded beaches, hidden coves, and quaint fishing villages along the way. Hiking the Path of the Gods is also a stunning experience, offering breathtaking views of the coastline and surrounding mountains. Ravello is another charming hilltop village known for its stunning villas, gardens, and panoramic views. Don't forget to try the local cuisine, featuring fresh seafood, homemade pasta, and locally grown fruits and vegetables. And, of course, relax on the beaches, like Spiaggia Grande in Positano and Marina Grande in Amalfi.

Towns

The towns along the Amalfi Coast are charming and picturesque and offer a unique glimpse into the local way of life. The towns are perched on the cliffs overlooking the sea, and each one has its own distinct character and charm. The town of Amalfi is the largest town and serves as the cultural and economic center of the region. The town boasts a beautiful cathedral, a picturesque harbor, and a bustling town center filled with shops and restaurants. The town of Positano is known for its colorful houses, winding streets, and stunning views of the sea. The town is popular with tourists and is home to several high-end boutiques and luxury hotels. The town of Ravello is perched on a hilltop and is known for its stunning villas, lush gardens, and historical landmarks. The town also hosts an annual music festival that attracts visitors from around the world. The towns along the Amalfi Coast are vibrant and offer a unique blend of history, culture, and natural beauty that is sure to captivate visitors.

Amalfi

Map Coordinates: 40.6340° N, 14.6027° E

Amalfi town is famous for its Duomo di Sant'Andrea, a stunning cathedral that dates back to the 9th century. The town is also known for its winding streets, quaint shops, and excellent seafood restaurants. Visitors to Amalfi town can enjoy a stroll along the waterfront promenade, take a boat tour along the Coast, or simply relax on the beach and soak up the sun. The town is easily accessible by bus or ferry from other towns along the Coast, including Positano and Sorrento.

Positano

Map Coordinates: 40.6281° N, 14.4850° E

Positano is a small, picturesque town located on the Amalfi Coast in southern Italy. It is known for its colorful cliffside houses, stunning beaches, and charming streets. Positano is a popular destination for tourists due to its beautiful scenery, luxurious resorts, and excellent shopping and dining options. Visitors to Positano can enjoy strolling through the narrow streets, visiting the town's many art galleries and boutiques, or relaxing on one of its beautiful beaches, such as Spiaggia Grande or Fornillo. The town also offers a number of hiking trails that provide stunning views of the Coast and the surrounding countryside.

Ravello

Map Coordinates: 40.6492° N, 14.6117° E

Ravello is a charming hilltop town situated on the Amalfi Coast in southern Italy. Known for its stunning views, historic villas, and beautiful gardens, Ravello is a popular destination for tourists looking to experience the beauty and tranquility of the Amalfi Coast. The town is home to lots of historic landmarks, including the 11th-century Duomo di Ravello and the stunning Villa Rufolo, which features beautiful gardens and panoramic views of the Coast.

Praiano

Map Coordinates: 40.6117° N, 14.5335° E

Praiano is a beautiful coastal town located on the Amalfi Coast in southern Italy. It is situated between the towns of Positano and Amalfi and offers stunning views of the Mediterranean Sea. Praiano is known for its peaceful atmosphere, beautiful beaches, and charming streets lined with colorful houses. The town's main attractions include the 16th-century Church of San Gennaro, which features beautiful frescoes and stunning views of the Coast, and Praia Beach, which is one of the most beautiful beaches on the Amalfi Coast.

Maiori

Map Coordinates: 40.6512° N, 14.6434° E

This seaside town is one of the largest on the Amalfi Coast and is known for its long beach, historic castle, and charming old town. Maiori's main attraction is the beautiful Cathedral of Santa Maria a Mare, which dates back to the 9th century and features beautiful Byzantine mosaics. The town also offers several other historic landmarks, such as the 12th-century Castle of San Nicola de Thoro-Plano and the Torre Normanna, a medieval tower that offers stunning views of the Coast.

Atrani

Map Coordinates: 40.6358° N, 14.6086° E

It is a short distance away from the larger town of Amalfi and offers stunning views of the Mediterranean Sea. Atrani is known for its charming, narrow streets, beautiful historic landmarks, and relaxed atmosphere. The town's main attraction is the 13th-century Church of San Salvatore de' Birecto, which features beautiful Byzantine-style architecture and stunning frescoes.

Cetara

Map Coordinates: 40.6498° N, 14.7000° E

It is situated between the towns of Maiori and Vietri sul Mare and is known for its picturesque harbor, colorful buildings, and delicious seafood. Cetara is a small town that is often overlooked by tourists, making it a great place to escape the crowds and experience the authentic charm of the Amalfi Coast.

BEACHES ON AMALFI COAST

The Amalfi Coast in Italy is known for its beautiful coastline and stunning beaches. One of the most incredible things about the Amalfi Coast beaches is their crystal-clear waters. The warm, inviting waters of the Mediterranean are perfect for swimming, and the surrounding cliffs and lush vegetation make for a picturesque backdrop. Visitors can relax on the beach and soak up the sun or take a mind-refreshing dip in the sea. Another feature that sets the Amalfi Coast beaches apart is their stunning natural scenery. The coastline is dotted with hidden coves and inlets, framed by dramatic cliffs and rugged rock formations. The beaches are often nestled in secluded bays, accessible only by boat or a winding footpath, adding to their sense of exclusivity and charm.

Marina Grande Beach

Address: Via Marina Grande, 270, 80076 Capri NA, Italy

Map Coordinates: 40.5573° N, 14.2361° E

Located in Amalfi, this pebble beach is one of the largest on the Amalfi Coast and is surrounded by colorful buildings and boats.

Fornillo Beach

Address: 24.2 km away from its center, the city of Salerno

Map Coordinates: 40.6264° N, 14.4822° E

This secluded beach is located in the town of Positano and is accessed via a scenic path through olive groves and lemon trees.

Spiaggia Grande

Address: adjacent to Marina Grande, Positano's port, Italy

Map Coordinates: 40° 38' 1.356" N, 14° 36' 10.116" E

Also located in Positano, this beach is known for its crystal-clear water and is a popular spot for swimming and sunbathing.

Arienzo Beach

Address: Arienzo 16 84017 Positano SA, Italy

Map Coordinates: 40.6268° N, 14.4959° E

This private beach is located just outside of Positano and is accessible via boat or a steep staircase. It offers stunning views of the coastline and is a great spot for snorkeling.

Fiordo Di Furore Beach

Address: Via Marina di Praia, 84010 Furore SA, Italy

Map Coordinates: 40° 36' 55.2024" N/ 14° 33' 5.1588" E

This pebble beach is located in the small town of Furore and is surrounded by high cliffs and crystal-clear water.

Santa Croce Beach

Address: Santa Croce Beach, Beach in Amalfi Coast, Italy.

Map Coordinates: 40° 37' 28.722" N and 14° 35' 9.2292" E

This secluded beach is located in the town of Maiori and is known for its clear blue water and stunning scenery.

La Marinella Beach

Address: Praiano, SA, Italy

Map Coordinates: 44° 07' 45.984" N, 8° 15' 47.196" E

Located in the town of Praiano, this small beach is surrounded by rocky cliffs and is a great spot for snorkeling and swimming.

HISTORIC SITES OF AMALFI COAST

The Amalfi Coast in Italy is a UNESCO World Heritage Site and is home to numerous historical sites.

Amalfi Cathedral:

Address: Piazza Duomo, 1, 84011 Amalfi SA, Italy

Opening hours & days: 10:00 am to 6:00 pm (Monday to Sunday)

Map Coordinates: 40.6345° N, 14.6030° E

Located in the town of Amalfi, this cathedral was built in the 9th century and featured a mix of architectural styles, including Byzantine, Romanesque, and Gothic.

Villa Rufolo:

Address: Piazza Duomo, 1, 84010 Ravello SA, Italy

Opening hours & days: 9 am–4:30 pm (Monday to Sunday)

Map Coordinates: 40.6490° N, 14.6120° E

This medieval villa in the town of Ravello was built in the 13th century and featured beautiful gardens and stunning views of the coastline.

Villa Cimbrone:

Address: Hotel Villa Cimbrone. Via S. Chiara, 26 - 84010 Ravello (Sa) Italy

Opening hours & days: 9 am–4:30 pm (Monday to Sunday)

Map Coordinates: 40.6441° N, 14.6110° E

Also located in Ravello, this 11th-century villa is famous for its stunning Terrace of Infinity, which offers panoramic views of the Amalfi Coast.

Pompeii:

Address: Via Villa dei Misteri, 2, 80045 Pompeii, Naples

Opening hours & days: 9 am–5:30 pm (Monday to Sunday)

Map Coordinates: 40.7462° N, 14.4989° E

While not technically located on the Amalfi Coast, the ancient city of Pompeii is only a short drive away and is definitely worth a visit. Pompeii- the old city was completely ruined by the violent eruption of Vesuvius in AD 79 and has been preserved in its original state.

Furore Fjord:

Address: Via Marina di Praia 2, 84010, Furore Italy

Opening hours & days: 24 hrs. (Monday to Sunday)

Map Coordinates: 40°37'17"N 14°32'58"E

While not a historic site per se, this stunning fjord located between Amalfi and Positano is a natural wonder and is definitely worth seeing.

GARDENS IN THE AMALFI COAST

The Amalfi Coast is known not only for its stunning sea views and picturesque towns but also for its beautiful gardens. Here are some of the most famous gardens in the region:

Villa Cimbrone Gardens (Ravello):

Address: Via Santa Chiara, 26, 84010 Ravello SA, Italy

Opening hours & days: 9 am–5 pm (Monday to Sunday)

Map Coordinates: 40.6423° N, 14.6102° E

These breathtaking gardens are situated on a clifftop overlooking the sea and offer stunning views of the Coast. The gardens are home to a variety of flora and fauna, including roses, geraniums, and lemon trees. Visitors can also explore the Temple of Bacchus and the Belvedere of Infinity, a terrace that offers sweeping views of the Coast.

Villa Rufolo Gardens (Ravello):

Address: Piazza Duomo, 1, 84010 Ravello SA, Italy

Opening hours & days: 9 am–6 pm (Monday to Sunday)

Map Coordinates: 40° 38' 57.3" N, 14° 36' 41.868" E

Located in the historic town of Ravello, the Villa Rufolo Gardens are a must-visit destination for any garden lover. The gardens feature a variety of Mediterranean plants, as well as fountains, terraces, and panoramic views of the sea.

Villa San Michele Gardens (Capri):

Address: Viale Axel Munthe, 34, 80071 Anacapri NA, Italy

Opening hours & days: 9 am–4:30 pm (Monday to Sunday)

Map Coordinates: 41.7403° N, 14.2371° E

Situated on the island of Capri, the Villa San Michele Gardens is a beautiful oasis of tranquility. Created by the Swedish physician Axel Munthe, the gardens feature a variety of Mediterranean plants, as well as ancient ruins and stunning sea views.

Whether you're a garden enthusiast or simply looking for a peaceful and calming escape from the hustle and bustle of the Coast, the gardens of the Amalfi Coast are sure to enchant and delight.

CHAPTER 5

FOOD AND DRINK

From fresh seafood to hearty pasta dishes, the Amalfi Coast has a variety of local dishes that are sure to delight any foodie.

Spaghetti Alle Vongole

One of the most amazing dishes of the Amalfi Coast is the spaghetti alle vongole. This dish consists of spaghetti pasta cooked in a savory clam sauce made with garlic, white wine, olive oil, and fresh clams. The pasta is cooked until it's al dente and then mixed with the clam sauce to create a deliciously flavorful dish that is both light and filling.

Baccalà Alla Napoletana

Another popular seafood dish found on the Amalfi Coast is the baccalà alla Napoletana. This dish features salted cod that has been soaked in water for several days to remove the excess salt. The cod is then cooked in a tomato sauce with garlic, onions, and other herbs and spices. The dish is typically served with crispy bread or potatoes and is a staple in many Amalfi Coast households.

Pollo Alla Cacciatora

For those who prefer meat dishes, the region has several delicious options as well. One of the most famous meat dishes in the Amalfi Coast is the pollo alla cacciatora. This dish features chicken that has been marinated in a mixture of olive oil, garlic, herbs, and white wine. The chicken is then slow-cooked in a tomato sauce with onions, mushrooms, and other vegetables until it's tender and flavorful. Another popular meat dish is the salsicce e friarielli. This dish features sausages that have been cooked in a tomato sauce with friarielli, a type of bitter broccoli that is native to the region. The dish is often served with bread or polenta and is a hearty and satisfying meal.

Limoncello

No visit to the Amalfi Coast would be complete without trying the region's famous Limoncello. This sweet and tangy liqueur is made from lemons that are grown in the region and are often served as a digestif after meals. It's also used in many desserts and is a popular ingredient in cocktails.

Seafood

In addition to these popular dishes, the Amalfi Coast is also known for its fresh seafood, which can be found in many restaurants and markets throughout the region. Some of the most popular Amalfi seafood dishes include grilled octopus, fried calamari, and baked fish with lemon and herbs.

This Coast is also known for its variety of shellfish, including mussels, scallops, and oysters. These are typically served raw or cooked with garlic, parsley, and white wine, and they are often paired with a crisp, dry white wine from the region. One of the unique seafood dishes from the Amalfi Coast is Zuppa di Pesce, or fish soup. This dish is made with a variety of seafood, including fish, shellfish, and squid, which are cooked in a tomato-based broth with garlic, onions, and herbs. The result is a flavorful and hearty soup that is perfect for a chilly evening.

CAFÉ AND RESTAURANTS

La Sponda

Address: Via Cristoforo Colombo, 30 84017 Positano (SA) Italia

Opening hours & days: 11:30 am–9 pm (Monday to Sunday)

Map Coordinates: 40.5828° N, 14.4341° E

This Michelin-starred restaurant is located within the five-star hotel Le Sirenuse in Positano. La Sponda serves elegant Mediterranean cuisine, and the restaurant's romantic atmosphere, complete with candlelit tables and live music, makes it a favorite among visitors to the Amalfi Coast.

Ristorante Marina Grande

Address: Viale della Regione, 4, 84011 Amalfi SA, Italy

Opening hours & days: 12 pm–9:45 pm (Monday to Sunday)

Map Coordinates: 40.6337° N, 14.6036° E

This seafood-focused restaurant is located in the charming fishing village of Sorrento, overlooking the Marina Grande. With fresh seafood caught daily by local fishermen, Ristorante Marina Grande is a popular destination for visitors to the Amalfi Coast.

II Flauto Di Pan

Address: Villa Cimbrone, 26, Via Santa Chiara, 84010 Ravello SA, Italy

Opening hours & days: 7 pm–10 pm (Monday to Sunday)

Map Coordinates: 40.6441° N, 14.6110° E

This restaurant in Ravello is known for its stunning views of the coastline, as well as its delicious traditional Italian cuisine. Diners can enjoy handmade pasta dishes, grilled meats, and fresh seafood while taking in the breathtaking scenery.

Da Adolfo

Address: Via Laurito, 40, 84017 Positano SA, Italy

Opening hours & days: 12 pm–9:45 pm (Monday to Sunday)

Map Coordinates: 40.6224° N, 14.5073° E

This beachfront restaurant in Positano is a local favorite, and it's simple, the rustic menu features fresh fish and seafood caught by local fishermen. Diners can also enjoy the restaurant's private beach and boat service to and from Positano.

Pasticceria Pansa

Address: Piazza Duomo, 40, 84011 Amalfi SA, Italy

Opening hours & days: 7:30 am–1 am (Monday to Sunday)

Map Coordinates: 40.6342° N, 14.6028° E

This historic bakery in Amalfi has been serving delicious pastries and cakes since 1830. Visitors can enjoy local specialties such as tagliatelle and ricotta-filled pastries while soaking up the atmosphere of this charming coastal town.

Bar Buca Di Bacco

Address: P.za Amerigo Vespucci, 84017 Positano SA, Italy

Opening hours & days: 7 am–12 am (Monday to Sunday)

Map Coordinates: 43° 26' 43.9368" N, 79° 40' 13.404" W

This cafe and bar in Positano are known for their stunning views of the sea and colorful buildings that make the town famous. Visitors can enjoy a refreshing drink or light bite while taking in the picturesque surroundings.

CHAPTER 6

OUTDOOR ACTIVITIES

Travelers who visit the Amalfi Coast can experience a wide range of outdoor activities that allow them to immerse themselves in the region's natural beauty. From hiking along scenic trails to exploring secluded beaches, the Amalfi Coast has something to offer everyone. If you're an adventurous traveler looking for some adrenaline-pumping activities, you can try your hand at rock climbing or paragliding. The rugged cliffs and steep mountains of the region provide ideal terrain for these activities, and the panoramic views from the top are nothing short of spectacular.

Hiking:

The Amalfi Coast offers some incredible hiking trails that allow you to explore the natural beauty of the region. The most popular hiking trails include the Path of the Gods (Sentiero degli Dei), the Valle delle Ferriere, and the Path of the Three Churches.

Path of the Gods (Sentiero degli Dei):

This is one of the widely popular and scenic hiking trails on the Amalfi Coast. The trail runs along the ridge of the Lattari Mountains, offering breathtaking views of the sea and coastline below. The trail can be accessed from the towns of Agerola or Praiano and takes around 4-5 hours to complete.

Valle delle Ferriere:

This trail takes hikers through a lush, green valley filled with waterfalls, streams, and a variety of flora and fauna. The trail starts in the town of Scala and ends in the town of Amalfi, taking around 3-4 hours to complete.

Monte Tre Calli:

This trail takes hikers to the summit of Monte Tre Calli, one of the highest peaks on the Amalfi Coast. The trail offers stunning views of the coastline and surrounding countryside and takes around 4-5 hours to complete.

The Path of the Two Gulfs:

This trail connects the towns of Maiori and Minori, offering stunning views of both the Amalfi Coast and the Gulf of Salerno. The trail takes around 2-3 hours to complete, and it is suitable for hikers of all levels.

Punta Campanella:

This trail takes hikers to the tip of the Sorrento Peninsula, offering stunning views of the Bay of Naples and Capri Island. The trail starts in the town of Termini and takes around 3-4 hours to complete.

No matter which hiking trail you choose, be sure to bring plenty of water, wear sturdy shoes, and be prepared for the steep and rocky terrain that is common on the Amalfi Coast.

SCUBA DIVING:

If you're a fan of scuba diving, the Amalfi Coast has some excellent dive spots. You can explore underwater caves, shipwrecks, and marine life.

Isola di Li Galli:

This small island off the Coast of Positano is home to some of the best scuba diving spots on the Amalfi Coast. The waters here are crystal clear, and divers can explore underwater caves, swim through schools of fish, and encounter octopuses, lobsters, and other marine life.

Marina del Cantone:

This small fishing village near Sorrento is home to several excellent diving spots. The waters here are teeming with marine life, including schools of colorful fish, octopuses, and even the occasional sea turtle.

Capo di Conca:

This rocky promontory near Amalfi offers some of the most dramatic underwater scenery on the Amalfi Coast. Divers can explore underwater caves and tunnels, swim through schools of fish, and even encounter dolphins and whales in the deeper waters offshore.

Punta Campanella:

This rocky headland near Sorrento is home to several excellent diving spots, including the famous "Blue Grotto." Divers can explore underwater caves and tunnels, swim through schools of fish, and encounter sea urchins, starfish, and other marine life.

Punta di San Lorenzo:

This rocky point near Maiori offers some of the best visibility on the Amalfi Coast, with waters that are crystal clear even at depth. Divers can explore underwater cliffs and rock formations, swim through schools of fish, and encounter octopuses, moray eels, and other marine life.

It's important to note that scuba diving can be a dangerous sport and should only be attempted with the proper equipment and training. Be sure to research any diving operators carefully, and only work with reputable companies that have a track record of safety and reliability.

KAYAKING:

Rent a kayak and explore the Coast at your own pace. You can paddle to secluded beaches, coves, and caves.

Marina di Praia:

This small fishing village near Praiano is a popular spot for kayaking, with calm waters and plenty of scenic coastlines to explore. Kayakers can paddle past sea stacks, arches, and hidden coves and even stop for a swim or a picnic on one of the secluded beaches.

Furore Fjord:

This dramatic fjord near Furore is a must-visit for kayakers, with towering cliffs, turquoise waters, and plenty of hidden coves and sea caves to explore. Kayakers can paddle through the narrow inlet, past fishing villages and ancient watchtowers, and even stop for a swim in the crystal-clear waters.

Conca dei Marini:

This picturesque town near Amalfi is surrounded by some of the most beautiful and scenic coastlines in the region, and kayakers can explore hidden coves, sea caves, and secluded beaches along the way. The waters here are calm and clear, making it a great spot for beginner and intermediate kayakers.

Maiori:

This charming town near Salerno is a great base for kayaking adventures, with plenty of rental shops and guided tours available. Kayakers can paddle past scenic beaches, sea cliffs, and ancient watchtowers and even stop for a swim or a snorkel in the warm waters.

Capri Island:

While technically not part of the Amalfi Coast, the nearby island of Capri is a popular destination for kayakers, with crystal-clear waters and stunning coastal scenery. Kayakers can paddle past sea stacks, hidden coves, and even the famous Blue Grotto, a sea cave known for its otherworldly blue light.

Kayaking is a relatively safe and accessible activity, but it's still important to take proper precautions and follow safety guidelines. Always wear a life jacket, bring plenty of water and sunscreen, and be aware of tides, currents, and other potential hazards.

PARAGLIDING:

Take a tandem paragliding flight and experience the thrill of flying over the stunning Coast. This Coast is not known for its paragliding opportunities, as the steep and rugged terrain of the region can make it difficult to find suitable launch and landing sites. However, there are a few places in the area where paragliding is possible:

Castellammare di Stabia:

This town, located just south of the Amalfi Coast, is home to a paragliding school that offers tandem flights with experienced pilots. The flights take off from the slopes of Mount Faito, offering stunning views of the Bay of Naples and the surrounding countryside.

Mount Vesuvius:

This famous volcano, located near Naples, is a popular destination for paragliding enthusiasts. The launch site is located near the crater rim, and flights offer stunning views of the Bay of Naples and the surrounding area.

Salerno:

This city, located at the eastern end of the Amalfi Coast, is home to a paragliding school that offers tandem flights over the Coast and surrounding countryside. Flights take off from the hills behind the city and offer stunning views of the Gulf of Salerno and the surrounding hills.

Other Activities

Cycling: The Amalfi Coast offers some challenging but rewarding cycling routes that take you through picturesque towns, along the Coast, and up into the hills.

Beach hopping: The Amalfi Coast is home to some of the most stunning and beautiful beaches in Italy. Some of the best beaches include Fornillo Beach in Positano, Marina Grande Beach in Amalfi, and Fiordo di Furore Beach.

Boat tours: Take a boat tour and explore the stunning coastline from the sea. You can rent a boat or join a tour that will take you to some of the most beautiful spots along the Coast.

Rock climbing: If you're an experienced climber, the Amalfi Coast offers some fantastic rock climbing routes with stunning views of the coastline.

CHAPTER 7

THE SHOPPING EXPERIENCE

Shopping on the Amalfi Coast can be a delightful experience, with many unique stores and boutiques offering handmade crafts, ceramics, and artisanal products. You can find many stores selling beautiful handmade paper products, such as journals, cards, and bookmarks. Other popular souvenirs include ceramics, Limoncello (a traditional lemon liqueur), and local food products like olive oil and pasta. If you want to take some souvenirs back home for your family and friends, then here are some things that you should definitely consider:

Limoncello:

Limoncello is a sweet and tangy Italian liqueur that is made using lemon zest, alcohol, sugar, and water. It is a specialty of the Amalfi Coast, where the lemons are particularly fragrant and flavorful. The process of making Limoncello involves steeping lemon zest in alcohol for several weeks, which allows the natural oils and flavors to infuse into the liquid. The mixture is then strained and sweetened with a syrup made from sugar and water, resulting in a bright yellow liqueur that is often served chilled as an after-dinner digestif.

Ceramics:

Ceramics have been an important part of the cultural heritage of the Amalfi Coast for centuries. The region is home to many skilled ceramic artisans who produce a wide range of beautiful, handcrafted pieces that reflect the local traditions and landscapes. The tradition of ceramic-making on the Amalfi Coast dates back to the medieval era when Moorish potters settled in the region and began to produce ceramics using local clay. Over the centuries, the art of ceramic making was refined and expanded, with new techniques and designs being introduced.

Olive Oil:

The Amalfi Coast in Italy is famous for producing some of the highest-quality olive oil in the country. The region's ideal climate and fertile soil make it an ideal location for growing olives. The most common olive varieties grown on the Amalfi Coast include the Rotondella, the Piantone di Falerone, and the Ogliarola. These varieties produce an oil that is fruity, mild, and aromatic. Olive oil from the Amalfi Coast is made using traditional methods, with olives hand-picked and cold-pressed within 24 hours of harvest. This helps to preserve the flavor and quality of the oil. Olive oil from the Amalfi Coast has a unique flavor that is fruity, grassy, and slightly bitter. It is perfect for drizzling over salads or pasta or for dipping bread.

Leather Sandals:

Positano, a charming town on the Amalfi Coast, is renowned for its handmade leather sandals. These sandals are made by skilled artisans who use traditional techniques to create custom-fit shoes. The leather used for the sandals is of the highest quality, ensuring that the sandals are comfortable, durable, and long-lasting. These sandals come in various styles, from simple to elaborate designs with beads and embroidery, and are perfect for any occasion. The artisans in Positano can even customize the sandals to fit your feet perfectly, allowing maximum comfort and style. You can find these sandals in local shops and markets throughout the town or order them online and have them shipped to your doorstep.

Cameo Jewelry:

Torre del Greco, a small town on the Amalfi Coast, is renowned for its beautiful and intricate cameo jewelry. The town has a long history of producing this exquisite jewelry, dating back to the 15th century. The artisans in Torre del Greco use a variety of materials, including shells, coral, and precious stones, to create their intricate designs. Each piece is carefully carved by hand using traditional techniques, ensuring that it is of the highest quality. The designs often feature classical figures, landscapes, and animals, making each piece a unique work of art. The artisans in Torre del Greco can even customize the jewelry to your specifications, creating a unique piece that is tailored to your style.

Italian Wine:

The Amalfi Coast is famous for its beautiful landscapes and delicious food, but it's also known for its excellent Italian wines. The region's Mediterranean climate is perfect for growing two primary grape varieties, the white grape "Falanghina" and the red grape "Aglianico," which produce unique and flavorful wines. The wines of the Amalfi Coast come in various styles, including dry whites, rosés, and full-bodied reds. Some of the most well-known wines from the region include "Furore Bianco," "Ravello Rosso," and "Tramonti Rosso."

Local Honey:

Local honey from the Amalfi Coast is known for its unique taste and healing properties. It is said to have a variety of health benefits, including boosting immunity, improving digestion, and reducing inflammation. Local beekeepers often produce honey using traditional methods, which involve collecting honeycombs from hives in the mountains and hills surrounding the coastline.

Handmade Pasta:

Scialatielli and paccheri are two traditional pasta types that can be found in local markets and food shops. The traditional method of pasta-making in the region involves using durum wheat semolina and cold water, which mixed together by hand to create a dough. The dough is then rolled out by hand and cut into various shapes, including spaghetti, fettuccine, and ravioli. Handmade pasta is known for its unique flavor and texture, and it is often paired with locally sourced ingredients, such as fresh seafood, vegetables, and herbs. Some of the most popular pasta dishes in the region include spaghetti alle vongole (spaghetti with clams), linguine ai frutti di mare (linguine with seafood), and ravioli di ricotta e limone (ricotta and lemon ravioli).

Capodimonte Porcelain:

Capodimonte porcelain is a famous type of porcelain that is produced in the Campania region, including the Amalfi Coast. The art of Capodimonte porcelain production dates back to the 18th century when King Charles III of Naples founded the Royal Porcelain Factory in Capodimonte. The porcelain produced at the factory was known for its high quality and exquisite beauty.

Italian Leather Goods:

The Amalfi Coast is renowned for its high-quality Italian leather goods, including shoes, handbags, belts, and jackets. The leather used in these products is sourced from local tanneries and is known for its durability, softness, and beautiful texture. Skilled artisans craft the leather into a wide range of products using traditional techniques that have been passed down through generations.

FAMOUS MARKETS

The Amalfi Coast is home to several famous markets where you can find local produce, artisanal products, and souvenirs. Here are some of the most popular markets in the region:

Amalfi Street Market:

Address: Via Lungomare dei Cavalieri, 84011 Amalfi SA, Italy

Opening hours & days: 8 am - 1 pm (Monday to Saturday)

This bustling market in the town of Amalfi is held every day and offers a wide range of local products, including fresh fruits and vegetables, fish, cheese, and handmade crafts. You can also find clothing, shoes, and accessories, making it a great hub for bargain hunters. The Mercato di Amalfi, or Amalfi Market, is a popular open-air market located in the heart of the historic town of Amalfi on the Amalfi Coast. This market opens every day except Sundays and features a wide variety of local products, including fresh fruits and vegetables, seafood, meats, cheeses, and specialty items such as Limoncello and handmade pasta.

Mercato Di Positano:

Address: Via dei Mulini, Positano, SA, Italy

Opening hours & days: 8 am–1 pm (Monday to Sunday)

The Mercato di Positano, or Positano Market, is a vibrant open-air market located in the heart of the picturesque town of Positano on the Amalfi Coast. The market is held every Wednesday and features a wide variety of products, like fresh produce, fish, meat, cheeses, and specialty items such as Limoncello and handmade pasta. The market is a popular destination for both locals and tourists alike, offering a lively atmosphere and a chance to sample and purchase some of the region's most delicious and unique products. Vendors are friendly and knowledgeable, and many are happy to share their recipes and cooking tips with visitors.

Mercato Del Pesce Di Cetara:

Address: Piazza Martiri Ungheresi, 10, 84010 Cetara SA, Italy

Opening hours & days: 8 am–8:30 pm (Monday to Sunday)

If you're a seafood lover, be sure to visit the fish market in the town of Cetara, which is held every morning. The Mercato del Pesce di Cetara, or Cetara Fish Market, is a lively and colorful market located in the small fishing village of Cetara on the Amalfi Coast. The market is held every morning and features a wide range of fish and seafood caught by local fishermen.

Mercato Di Minori:

Address: Via Lama, 6, 84010 Minori SA, Italy

Opening hours & days: 7:30 am–8:30 pm (Monday to Sunday)

The market is held every Thursday and offers a wide range of fresh produce, meats, cheeses, and other food products, as well as handicrafts and souvenirs. All the visitors to the market can browse the stalls and sample a range of local specialties, including the region's famous lemons, which are used to make Limoncello and a variety of other dishes and drinks. Other popular items available at the market include fresh vegetables and fruits, such as tomatoes, zucchini, and figs, as well as cheeses and cured meats.

Mercato Dei Fiori Di Ravello:

Address: Via Papa Leone X, 84011 Amalfi SA, Italy

Opening hours & days: 8 am–8 pm (Monday to Sunday)

This flower market in the town of Ravello is held every Friday and features a stunning array of colorful blooms, including the region's famous bougainvillea. You can also find potted plants, herbs, and other gardening supplies.

SPECIALTY STORES

The Amalfi Coast is known for its unique and delicious specialty products, and there are several stores and markets where you can find these items. Here are some famous specialty stores on the Amalfi Coast:

Limoncello Di Capri:

Address: Via Roma, 85, 80073 Capri NA, Italy

Opening hours & days: 9:30 am–8 pm (Monday to Sunday)

This iconic lemon liqueur is a must-try when visiting the Amalfi Coast. Limoncello di Capri is a family-run business that has been producing high-quality Limoncello since 1906. You can visit their store on Capri Island and sample their various flavors of Limoncello, as well as other citrus-based products like lemon candies and marmalades.

Antica Salumeria Gambardella:

Address: Corso Italia, 38, 80067 Sorrento NA, Italy

Opening hours & days: 9 am–10 pm (Monday to Sunday)

This historic deli in Sorrento has been serving up the region's famous cured meats and cheeses since 1861. Antica Salumeria Gambardella is known for its high-quality products and friendly service, and you can find everything from prosciutto and salami to buffalo mozzarella and aged parmesan.

Ceramiche Cosmolena Di Margherita Di Palma:

Address: Via della Marra, 15, 84010 Ravello SA, Italy

Opening hours & days: 9 am–9 pm (Monday to Sunday)

This artisanal ceramics shop in Ravello produces beautiful and unique pottery using traditional techniques. The shop's owner, Margherita di Palma, creates each piece by hand and draws inspiration from the region's natural beauty and cultural heritage.

Azienda Agricola Furore:

Address: Via Ostaglio - Altimari, 11, 84131 Salerno SA, Italy

Opening hours & days: 8 am–7 pm (Monday to Sunday)

This family-owned winery in Furore produces some of the region's best wines using traditional methods and indigenous grape varieties. A visit to Azienda Agricola Furore includes a tour of the vineyard, a tasting of their various wines, and the opportunity to purchase bottles to take home.

CHAPTER 8

CULTURE AND ARTS

The Amalfi Coast isn't just a feast for the eyes; it's a cultural and artistic wonderland that will leave you breathless. As you explore this stunning coastline, you'll be transported back in time to the medieval and Renaissance eras, where you'll discover a treasure trove of historical and architectural gems. From the picturesque town of Ravello with its magnificent Villa Rufolo and stunning gardens to the breathtaking Cathedral of Amalfi, you'll be awed by the intricate mosaics, beautiful marble facades, and striking bell towers that dot the landscape.

But the Amalfi Coast isn't just about the past. It's also a vibrant hub of creativity and innovation, where music, theater, and dance flourish year-round. Immerse yourself in the region's lively arts scene, which includes an array of festivals and events such as the Ravello Festival, featuring classical and contemporary music performances, and the Amalfi Coast International Film Festival, showcasing the works of up-and-coming filmmakers from around the world. Whether you're an architecture buff, an art lover, or simply looking to experience the magic of this enchanting region, the Amalfi Coast offers a cultural and artistic experience like no other.

FESTIVALS

The Amalfi Coast is known for its vibrant festivals and celebrations throughout the year. Here are some of the most popular festivals and events in the region:

Ravello Festival:

Days of Festival: Beginning on the 17th of April and ending on the 20th of October.

The Ravello Festival, also known as the Ravello Music Festival, is a yearly music and arts festival held in the town of Ravello on the Amalfi Coast of Italy. The festival was founded in 1953 by the composer Richard Wagner's granddaughter, and it has since become one of the most important cultural events in Italy. The festival takes place over several weeks in the summer months, typically from late June to early September, and features a diverse program of music, dance, theater, and other performing arts. The festival's events are held in some of Ravello's most beautiful and historic venues, including the Villa Rufolo and the Belvedere of Villa Cimbrone.

Festa Di Sant'Andrea:

Days of Festival: November 30th.

The Festa di Sant'Andrea, also known as the Feast of St. Andrew, is an annual religious festival celebrated in the town of Amalfi on the Amalfi Coast of Italy. The festival takes place on the 30th of November, the feast day of Saint Andrew, who is the patron saint of Amalfi. The festival's celebrations include a procession through the streets of Amalfi, led by a statue of Saint Andrew carried by local residents. The procession is accompanied by music, dancing, and fireworks, and it ends with a mass at the town's cathedral.

Positano International Chamber Music Festival:

Days of Festival: Mid-July to early August

The Positano International Chamber Music Festival is an annual music festival held in the town of Positano on the Amalfi Coast of Italy. The festival was founded in 2000 by the Italian-American pianist and composer Jeffery Swann. The festival takes place over several weeks in the summer months, typically from mid-July to early August, and features a diverse program of classical music, jazz, and other musical genres. The festival's events are held in some of Positano's most beautiful and historic venues, including the Church of Santa Maria Assunta and the Hotel Palazzo Murat.

Lemon Festival:

Days of Festival: the 30th of September - the 1st of October.

The Lemon Festival, also known as the Festa del Limone, is an annual event held in the town of Menton, which is located near the border of Italy and France. Although it is not directly on the Amalfi Coast, the festival is a popular attraction for visitors to the region. The Lemon Festival takes place over two weeks in February and March, and it celebrates the town's heritage as a major producer of lemons. The festival features elaborate floats, parades, and decorations made entirely of lemons and oranges, as well as concerts, exhibitions, and other cultural events. One of the highlights of the Lemon Festival is the Golden Fruit Parade, which features floats decorated with thousands of lemons and oranges, as well as performers dressed in colorful costumes. The parade attracts visitors from all over the world and is a great opportunity to experience the unique culture and traditions of the Menton region.

Feast Of San Lorenzo:

Days of Festival: the 10th of August.

The Feast of San Lorenzo, also known as the Festival of Saint Lawrence, is an annual religious festival held in the town of Atrani on the Amalfi Coast of Italy. The festival is held in honor of Saint Lawrence, who is the patron saint of Atrani, and it takes place on the 10th of August every year. The Feast of San Lorenzo is a major event in Atrani, and it features a procession of the statue of Saint Lawrence through the town's narrow streets, accompanied by music, fireworks, and traditional local food and wine. The festival is also known for its colorful decorations, which include illuminated arches, lanterns, and flowers.

La Notte Bianca:

Days of Festival: One-day event held annually every October.

La Notte Bianca, which translates to "The White Night," is an annual event held in various cities and towns throughout Italy, including some locations on the Amalfi Coast. The event is typically held in late summer or early autumn and is an all-night festival that celebrates Italian culture, food, music, and art. During La Notte Bianca, participating towns and cities host a variety of events, including concerts, art exhibits, street performers, food and wine tastings, and other cultural activities. The festival is called "The White Night" because many of the events take place outdoors and continue into the early morning hours, creating a festive atmosphere that lasts throughout the night.

MUSEUMS

The Amalfi Coast is a region of Italy that is rich in history and culture; there are several museums in the area that showcase the art, archaeology, and history of the region. If you are a history buff who never misses the chance to visit museums, then the following are some great options to visit while you are on Amalfi Coast.

Museum Of Paper In Amalfi:

Address: Via delle Cartiere, 23, 84011 Amalfi SA, Italy

Opening hours & days: 10 am–7 pm (Monday to Sunday)

The Museum of Paper in Amalfi (Museo della Carta) is a museum dedicated to the history and production of paper in the town of Amalfi on the Amalfi Coast of Italy. The museum is made in an ancient paper mill that dates back to the 14th century, and it provides a fascinating insight into the history of paper-making.

The museum's exhibits trace the evolution of paper-making from ancient times to the current day, with a particular focus on the techniques and tools used in the production of handmade paper. Visitors can see how the paper-making process has evolved over time, from the use of traditional techniques such as pressing and drying to the modern machinery used in industrial production.

Diocesan Museum Of San Matteo:

Address: Largo Plebiscito, 12, 84121 Salerno SA, Italy

Opening hours & days: 9 am–1 pm (Thursday to Tuesday)

The museum's collection consists of a variety of religious artworks, including sculptures, paintings, and liturgical objects, spanning from the 12th to the 19th century. Some of the most significant pieces in the collection include a 12th-century wooden crucifix, a 14th-century sculpture of the Madonna and Child by Giovanni Pisano, and a 15th-century painting of the Annunciation by Beato Angelico.

Museo Archeologico Di Salerno:

Address: Via S. Benedetto, 28, 84122 Salerno SA, Italy

Opening hours & days: 9:00 am–7:30 pm (Tuesday to Sunday)

The Museo Archeologico Provinciale di Salerno (Salerno Provincial Archaeological Museum) is a museum located in the city of Salerno on the Amalfi Coast of Italy. The museum features a collection of artifacts from the ancient Greek and Roman periods, as well as exhibits that trace the history of the region from prehistoric times to the medieval period.

The museum's exhibits are diverse and include ancient Greek and Roman sculptures, ceramics, jewelry, and coins, as well as artifacts from the prehistoric period, such as tools and pottery. One of the museum's highlights is a collection of ancient Roman mosaics, which are beautifully preserved and provide a glimpse into the daily life and culture of the period.

Villa Romana:

Address: Via Capo di Piazza, 28, 84010 Minori SA, Italy

Opening hours & days: 9 am–7 pm (Monday to Sunday)

The Villa Romana is an ancient Roman villa located in the town of Minori on the Amalfi Coast of Italy. The villa was built during the 1st century AD and was discovered in the early 20th century during construction work in the town. The villa features a number of well-preserved frescoes, which provide a glimpse into the daily life and culture of ancient Rome. The frescoes depict a range of scenes, including mythological figures, landscapes, and domestic life, and are considered some of the finest examples of Roman frescoes in Italy.

Museo Della Ceramica:

Address: Palazzo Gavotti via Aonzo 9 17100 Savona Italy

Opening hours & days: 9 am-3 pm Tue-Sat, 9.30 am-1 pm Sun.

The Museo della Ceramica (Museum of Ceramics) is a museum located in the town of Vietri sul Mare on the Amalfi Coast of Italy. The museum features a collection of ceramics from the town, which is famous for its production of colorful and intricately designed ceramics. The museum's exhibits include a range of ceramics, from traditional pieces that date back to the 16th century to contemporary works by modern ceramicists. Visitors can see examples of plates, bowls, vases, and other decorative items, as well as learn about the history and techniques of ceramic production in the region.

Museo Mineralogico Campano:

Address: Via S. Ciro, 38, 80069 Vico Equense NA, Italy

Opening hours & days: 10 am–1 pm (Monday to Sunday)

The Museo Mineralogico Campano (Campanian Mineralogy Museum) is a museum located in the town of Vico

Equense on the Sorrentine Peninsula, which is part of the larger Campania region of Italy. The museum's collection consists of over 4,000 minerals and fossils from the local area and around the world.

The museum's exhibits showcase the geological history of the region, including the volcanic activity that shaped the landscape and produced many of the minerals in the collection. Visitors can see examples of rare and exotic minerals, as well as fossils of prehistoric animals and plants. The museum's displays also highlight the various uses of minerals, such as in jewelry and industrial processes.

ART GALLERIES

The Amalfi Coast has also been a source of inspiration for artists and artisans for centuries. There are several art galleries in the region where visitors can see and purchase local artwork. Some of the great art galleries that you can find on this Coast include:

Ceramiche D'arte Carmela:

Address: Via dei Rufolo, 16, 84010 Ravello SA, Italy

Opening and Closing time: 8 am–10 pm (Monday to Sunday)

Ceramiche d'Arte Carmela is a well-known ceramic workshop and store located in the town of Positano on the Amalfi Coast of Italy. The shop is owned by Carmela and her family, who have been making traditional ceramics in Positano for several generations.

The ceramics produced at Ceramiche d'Arte Carmela are handmade and painted using traditional techniques that have been passed down through the family. The shop offers a variety of products, including plates, bowls, vases, tiles, and other decorative items, all adorned with colorful designs inspired by the local scenery and culture. Carmela and her family take great pride in their work, and visitors to the shop can see the artisans at work, creating the ceramics by hand. The shop is also a popular destination for tourists looking for unique and authentic souvenirs to take home from their travels.

Studio Maresca:

Address: Corso Vittorio Emanuele II, 129, 80011 Acerra NA, Italy

Opening and Closing time: 3:00 pm - 7:00 pm (Monday to Friday)

Studio Maresca is a contemporary art gallery located in the city of Naples, Italy. The gallery was founded in 2007 by Raffaele Maresca and has since become a prominent destination for contemporary art enthusiasts. The gallery's mission is to showcase the work of both established and emerging contemporary artists, with a focus on promoting contemporary art from southern Italy.

Ravello Arte:

Address: Via Roma, 10, 84010 Ravello SA, Italy

Opening and Closing time: 10 am–6 pm (Monday to Sunday)

Ravello Arte is an art gallery located in the town of Ravello, which is situated on the Amalfi Coast of Italy. The gallery was founded in 1961 and has since become a well-known destination for art lovers visiting the Amalfi Coast. Ravello Arte's mission is to promote the work of both local and international artists, with a focus on contemporary art.

La Scuderia Del Duca:

Address: Largo cesareo console, 8,Via Cardinale Marino del Giudice, Piazza Duomo, 41, Piazza Duomo, 31, 84011 Amalfi SA, Italy

Opening and Closing time: 10 am–2 pm (Monday to Saturday)

La Scuderia del Duca is a cultural center located in the city of Naples, Italy. The center is housed in a beautiful historic building that was once a horse stable for the Duke of Naples. La Scuderia del Duca's mission is to promote and preserve the cultural heritage of Naples, with a focus on music, art, and literature. The center offers a range of cultural events and activities, including concerts, art exhibitions, book presentations, and workshops. The center is particularly known for its music program, which features a range of classical and contemporary music performances throughout the year. La Scuderia del Duca also hosts a number of literary events, including readings and book signings by local and international authors.

La Bottega Dell'artigiano:

Address: Funo, Argelato Metropolitan City of Bologna, Italy

Opening and Closing time: 8 am–4:30 pm (Monday to Friday)

La Bottega dell'Artigiano is a small artisan shop located in the town of Ravello on the Amalfi Coast of Italy. The shop is dedicated to promoting and preserving the traditional art of ceramics, which has a rich history in the region. The shop features a range of handcrafted ceramic products, including plates, bowls, vases, and decorative items. All of the products are made by local artisans using traditional techniques, and each piece is unique and beautifully crafted.

MUSIC

The Amalfi Coast has a rich musical tradition that reflects the region's history and culture. Traditional folk music and dance are still performed at festivals and celebrations throughout the region, and there are also several venues where visitors can enjoy live music performances. Some of the most popular types of music on the Amalfi Coast are:

Tarantella: This traditional folk dance is performed throughout southern Italy and is often accompanied by lively accordion music.

Neapolitan songs: The city of Naples has a rich musical tradition, and many popular Italian songs have their roots in the region. Neapolitan songs are often characterized by their romantic lyrics and melodic tunes.

Opera: Italy is known for its contributions to opera, and the Amalfi Coast is no exception. The city of Salerno has a thriving opera scene, and there are several venues throughout the region where visitors can enjoy live performances.

Jazz: There are several jazz clubs and festivals in the Amalfi Coast region, including the jazz on the Rocks festival in Positano and the Ravello Festival.

Contemporary music: The Amalfi Coast has a vibrant contemporary music scene, with several local bands and performers showcasing a range of styles, from rock and pop to electronic and experimental music.

CHAPTER 9

PRACTICAL INFORMATION

The Amalfi Coast is located in Italy, which is a member of the EU-European Union and the Schengen Area. Depending on your own nationality and the length of your stay, you may or may not need a visa to visit the Amalfi Coast. Here is an overview of the visa requirements for visitors to Italy:

- **Visa-Free Access:**

Citizens of the European Union, as well as citizens of many other countries, do not need a visa to visit Italy for up to 90 days. This includes citizens of the United States, Canada, Australia, New Zealand, and Japan, among others.

- **Visa Required:**

Citizens of some countries, such as China, India, and Russia, require a visa to visit Italy. Visitors from these countries should check with the Italian embassy or consulate in their respective home country for more information on the application process for the visa.

- **Long-Term Stay:**

Visitors who plan to stay in Italy for more than 90 days will need to apply for a long-term visa, which is also known as a National visa or D visa. This type of visa allows visitors to stay in Italy for up to one year and may require additional documentation and a different application process.

It is important to note that visa requirements can change at any time, and visitors should always check with the Italian embassy or consulate in their home country for the latest information. Additionally, visitors may be required to show proof of travel insurance and sufficient funds for their stay when entering Italy.

Charges For Italian Visa

The charges for an Italian visa vary depending on the type of visa applied for and the nationality of the applicant. Here are some general guidelines:

Short-term visa (up to 90 days): The fee for a short-term Italian visa is currently €80 for most nationalities. However, the fee may be lower or waived for certain categories, such as children under six years old, family members of EU citizens, and students or researchers participating in certain programs.

Long-term visa (more than 90 days): The fee for a long-term Italian visa is currently €116. However, the fee may be lower or waived for certain categories, such as family members of EU citizens, students, and researchers participating in certain programs.

It is important to note that these fees are subject to change and may vary depending on the exchange rate. Additionally, some embassies or consulates may charge additional fees for services such as express processing or document authentication. Visitors should check with the Italian embassy or consulate in their home country for the latest fee information and payment methods.

CURRENCY OF AMALFI COAST

The currency used in the Amalfi Coast, as well as in the rest of Italy, is the Euro (EUR). The EUR is divided into 100 cents, and there are coins with values of 1, 2, 5, 10, 20, and 50 cents, along with 1 and 2 Euro coins. Banknotes in EUR are available with values of 5 to 10, 20, 50, 100, 200, and 500 Euro.

Money Exchange Services

Visitors to the Amalfi Coast can exchange their currency at banks, exchange offices, and some hotels. ATMs are also widely available on the Amalfi Coast, and most major credit cards are accepted at hotels, restaurants, and shops.

Banks: Banks offer the most secure and reliable option for exchanging currency. They usually offer competitive exchange rates but may charge a commission or transaction fee.

Exchange offices: Exchange offices can be found in tourist areas and offer convenient exchange services. However, they may offer less favorable exchange rates than banks and may charge a commission or transaction fee.

Hotels: Some hotels on the Amalfi Coast may offer currency exchange services, but they may not offer the best exchange rates.

ATMs: ATMs are widely available in the Amalfi Coast and allow you to withdraw cash in the local currency using your debit or credit card. However, be aware that the banks may charge a foreign transaction fee or currency conversion fee.

It is crucial to shop around and compare exchange rates and fees before exchanging money. Additionally, be sure to exchange money at reputable locations to avoid scams or counterfeit currency.

Weather

The weather on the Amalfi Coast is typically Mediterranean, which is hot and dry summers and mild winters. The best time to visit this Coast is during the months of

May to September when the temperatures range from 22°C to 30°C (72°F to 86°F), and there is very little rainfall. In the summer months, the sea temperature is warm enough for swimming, and visitors can enjoy long, sunny days. In contrast, the winter months are cooler, with temperatures ranging from 8°C to 16°C (46°F to 60°F), and there is more rainfall.

Language

Italian is the official language of the Amalfi Coast and the rest of Italy. However, due to the area's popularity as a tourist destination, many locals and businesses on the Amalfi Coast also speak English, especially in tourist areas. In addition, some locals may also speak other languages, such as German, French, and Spanish, particularly those who work in the tourism industry. It is always helpful to learn some basic Italian phrases when visiting the Amalfi Coast, as this can help you communicate with locals and enhance your overall experience.

SAFETY AND HEALTH

Emergency services, medical facilities, travel insurance, and common scams are important considerations for anyone traveling to the Amalfi Coast. Here is a detailed overview of all the services you can avail for your own personal safety and health.

Emergency Services:

In Italy, the national emergency number is 112. This number can be used to contact emergency services, including ambulance, fire, and police. It is imperative to note that the emergency services in Italy may not always have English-speaking operators, so it is a good idea to learn some basic Italian phrases to use in case of an emergency.

In case of a medical emergency, the ambulance service in Italy is provided by the National Health Service (Servizio Sanitario Nazionale, or SSN). The SSN provides free emergency medical care to all people who are in need, regardless of their nationality or insurance status. However, it is important to note that non-urgent medical care may require payment. If you need to contact the police in Italy, you can call the Carabinieri, which is the national police force. They are responsible for maintaining public order and investigating crimes. In addition to the Carabinieri, there is also the Polizia di Stato, which is responsible for patrolling the streets and maintaining public safety.

In case of a fire, you can call the Vigili del Fuoco, which is the national fire service in Italy. They are responsible for extinguishing fires and rescuing people from dangerous situations.

- Carabinieri (national police force): 112 or 113
- Polizia di Stato (local police force): 113
- Vigili del Fuoco (fire department): 115
- Emergenza Sanitaria (emergency medical services): 118

Medical Facilities:

There are several medical facilities on the Amalfi Coast, including hospitals, clinics, and pharmacies. The larger towns, such as Amalfi and Positano, have hospitals with emergency departments. It's important to note that medical care in Italy can be expensive for foreigners, so it's recommended to have travel insurance.

Travel Insurance:

It's highly recommended to have travel insurance when visiting the Amalfi Coast. This can help cover medical expenses, emergency medical evacuation, and trip cancellations or interruptions. Make sure to carefully read the terms and conditions of your travel insurance policy and to carry proof of travel insurance with you at all times.

Common Scams:

Unfortunately, scams can occur in any tourist destination, and the Amalfi Coast is no exception. Some common scams to watch out for include:

- Overcharging for goods or services, particularly in tourist areas.
- Pickpocketing and theft in crowded areas.

- "Friendly" strangers who offer to show you around or give you a ride, only to ask for money or steal from you.
- Fake police officers ask for your identification and wallet or for you to pay a "fine."

To avoid scams, be cautious of strangers who approach you, especially if they are offering you something for free or asking for money. Always keep an eye on your belongings and be wary of pickpockets in crowded areas. It's also a good idea to research common scams in the area before you arrive and to ask locals or your hotel for advice.

SUSTAINABILITY AND RESPONSI-
BLE TOURISM

Amalfi coast is a treasure with its magnificent ecosystems. This natural beauty has to be protected and preserved. Since thousands of people visit this Coast every season, it was important to go the extra mile to keep the Amalfi Coast clean, pollution-free, and preserved in its natural state. For this reason, the Italian government has started several sustainability and responsible tourism initiatives. Through those initiatives, the city administration encourages the visitors to support them in protecting the Coast.

Waste management: Many businesses on the Amalfi Coast have implemented recycling programs and use eco-friendly products to reduce waste. Visitors are encouraged to properly dispose of their waste and to recycle when possible.

Energy conservation: Many hotels and guesthouses on the Amalfi Coast have implemented energy-saving practices, like using renewable energy sources and reducing water usage. Visitors are encouraged to stay in these types of accommodations to support sustainable tourism.

Sustainable transportation: The local government encourages visitors to use public transportation, such as buses and ferries, to reduce carbon emissions and traffic congestion. There are also bike rental services available for those who want to explore the area on two wheels.

Conservation of natural and cultural heritage: The Amalfi Coast is a UNESCO World Heritage Site, and there are efforts to preserve the natural and cultural heritage of the area. Visitors are encouraged to respect the environment and cultural sites and not to litter or damage them.

Support for local businesses: Visitors are encouraged to support local businesses, such as family-owned restaurants and shops. This helps to boost the local economy and promotes sustainable tourism.

Education and awareness: There are educational programs and initiatives in place to raise awareness about sustainable and responsible tourism practices among visitors and locals.

By promoting sustainability and responsible tourism practices, the Amalfi Coast aims to protect its natural and cultural heritage while also promoting economic growth and community development. Visitors can play a role in supporting these initiatives by choosing eco-friendly accommodations, using public transportation, and supporting local businesses.

Overall, the responsible tourism initiatives on the Amalfi Coast aim to promote sustainable tourism practices that benefit both the environment and the local community. By following these initiatives, visitors can help to preserve the beauty and cultural heritage of the area for future generations to enjoy.

CHAPTER 10

FAQ

Q: Where is the Amalfi Coast located?

A: The Amalfi Coast is located on the southern Coast of Italy, in the Campania region.

Q: What is the best time of the year to visit the Amalfi Coast?

A: The best time to visit the Amalfi Coast is from late spring (May) to early autumn (September/October). The weather is warm and sunny during this time, and the sea is calm.

Q: How do I get to the Amalfi Coast?

A: The nearest airport to the Amalfi Coast is Naples International Airport, which is well-connected to major European cities. From Naples, you can take a taxi, hire a private car, or take a bus or a train to reach the Amalfi Coast.

Q: What are the top attractions on the Amalfi Coast?

A: The Amalfi Coast is known for its beautiful coastal towns, such as Positano, Amalfi, and Ravello. Other top attractions include the Path of the Gods hiking trail, the historic Villa Rufolo and Villa Cimbrone, and the beautiful beaches and coves.

Q: What is the food like on the Amalfi Coast?

A: The Amalfi Coast is famous for its delicious Mediterranean cuisine, which includes fresh seafood, pasta dishes, and locally grown produce. Some of the must-try dishes include spaghetti alle vongole (spaghetti with clams), Insalata di mare (seafood salad), and Limoncello (lemon liqueur).

Q: Which currency can I use on the Amalfi Coast?

A: The currency used in Italy, including the Amalfi Coast, is the Euro (€).

Q: What is the language spoken on the Amalfi Coast?

A: The official language of Italy is Italian, and this is the primary language spoken on the Amalfi Coast. However, many people in the tourist industry speak English, especially in the larger towns.

Q: Is it safe to travel to the Amalfi Coast?

A: Yes, the Amalfi Coast is generally considered a safe destination for travelers. However, as with any tourist destination, it is important to take precautions against theft and stay aware of your surroundings. It is also important to follow local rules and customs, especially when visiting churches and other religious sites.

CONCLUSION

As you come to the end of this travel guide, we hope that you have been inspired to visit the stunning Amalfi Coast. From the colorful towns perched on cliffs to the crystal-clear and blue waters of the Tyrrhenian Sea, this coastline is a true gem of Italy.

Whether you are looking for a nice and romantic getaway, an adventure-filled vacation, or simply a chance to relax and enjoy some of the most beautiful scenery in the world, the Amalfi Coast has something for everyone.

So go ahead, pack your bags, and set off on a journey of a lifetime to experience the enchanting beauty of the Amalfi Coast. Trust us; it will be a trip you will never forget!

Made in the USA
Middletown, DE
08 July 2023

34736782R00070